a diary – given to you

a diary - given to you

a story through poetry and prose

Karolina Valentina

ISBN: 978-0-578-94752-5

For Lydia.

*To picking up that 500-page journal and
always coming back.*

To my readers,

Ever since I was little, I have kept journals. My thoughts were nothing but many and I found myself in conjunction with the words on the pages. It was a means of escape and healing, but also of homage – placing my emotions in a time and space on paper - forever imprinted.

Sadly, like with many things, life gets in the way, and I stopped writing for a long time. It is when I found myself absolutely lost and broken that I came back to writing and allowed myself to feel everything and anything.

So here it is - I give you a piece of me through poetry.

A diary - given to you.

I hope my words resonate with you, even if my story differs from yours.

All my love,
Karolina Valentina

a diary – given to you

The Poet

"Why do you write? he asked.
So I can take my love for you and give it to
the world, I reply.
Because you won't take it from me."

-

Lang Leav

a diary – given to you

to write

It's paradoxical really.

There are moments where,
I don't miss you at all
And doubt if you ever loved me at all.

But then slowly,
Then all at once,

I know you loved me.
Deeply and most of all.

I'll have to write,
I'll have to write to feel it all.

somewhere in the middle

It's easy to write about beginnings —
Endings too.

I remember every detail
From day,
To weather,
To color,
To sweater.

I remember you.

But I reach for the middle
For those memories left.

Maybe we lost ourselves somewhere in the
middle.
Somewhere between all the chaos,
Somewhere between the hate
And, despair.

Somewhere in the middle
Maybe I'll find us there.

a diary – given to you

a diary – given to you

a diary – given to you

-
Living Together

a diary – given to you

a diary – given to you

morning tunes

Goooooodmorning, my love
Goooodmorning, my baaaaaby
Goooodmorning, my looove
Mmmm
Goooodmorning, my baaaby

You chuckle and laugh all at once.
God, you have an awful voice, you say.
But I love you all the more for it.

Sing it again.

Okay, ready?

Goooooodmorning, my love
Goooodmorning, my baaaaaby
Goooodmorning, my looove
Mmmm
Goooodmorning, my baaaby

a diary – given to you

blue chair

Slowly, I toss the blanket over
Place my feet on the wooden floor
One step after the other
I walk towards the kitchen door.

Open the cupboard,
Grab my favorite cup
K-cup in
And listen to the hissing of the machine.

Sit down in our blue chair,
Book in one hand,
Coffee in the other
Tired eyes
I read.

And then it rings.

a diary – given to you

I rush to the bedroom. Tiptoeing.
Kiss your cheek and forehead too.

Good morning, mein Herz.

Your tired eyes barely open
You pull me close
You look at me and mutter:

> *I love you*
> *Do you know that?*
> *I love waking up to you.*
> *I hope you'll never forget that.*
> *I love you.*

And we drift to sleep a little more.

lemon cupcakes – 2 and 2

On Sundays, I would make lemon
cupcakes.
Okay, Mondays too.
Maybe on Tuesdays, Wednesdays, and
Thursdays too.

Just a snack —
Or two.
We devoured them
Together —
Just us two

Sometimes, your friends would eat them
too.

My lemon cupcakes.
I really miss them too…

a diary – given to you

a diary – given to you

a diary – given to you

-

Dance. Dance. Dance.

a diary – given to you

interview

When I met you,
You were —

Different.
Still young
Craving danger and excitement
Not paying attention to the consequences

But you grew.

In that life, you spent your days
Drinking, smoking, selling
Fucking random girls too.
Isn't that what youth and excitement does
to you?

But you grew.

Now across from each other.
We practice for your interview.

I'm so excited for you.

---

a diary – given to you

Say this instead.
Word it this way.
Maybe leave that out.

Use your charm.
You know how too.

I move your chair.
Sit on your lap.
Kiss you and tell you:

> *I believe in you.*
> *I'll be in the other room.*

No. No.
Stay here.
I like having you here.

And it begins.

You breathe in and out.
Look at me
And mouth:

Thank you.

investment

They haven't reached out.

I'm sure they will.
Maybe they're just busy.
Besides, if they don't want you.
It's their loss.

You sigh.

I think you should reach out.
Nothing too overbearing.
Say you want an update.
That won't hurt.

Can you help me write it?

congratulations

Hey —
Apologies for the late reply.
We've been very busy.

You are on the alpha team.
Congratulations.

We look at each other.
Then at the screen.
Then at each other.

I scream.

AAAAAAAH
CONGRATULATIONS!
SEE, I KNEW IT.

I'M SO PROUD OF YOU!
AAAHSHSHDHS

You laugh.
Wide smile.
I grab your hand.

Let's dance.

a diary – given to you

dance dance dance

Bring you to the bedroom.
Move the workout mat away.

Lights.
Camera.
Action.

Dance. Dance. Dance.

You flick the lights on and off.
Disco time during Corona time?

That'll do.

I jump around.
You dance and sing.
We laugh and kiss.

Dance some more.

CONGRATULATIONS, I say.

I LOVE YOU!
I LOVE YOU TOO!
I love you.
I love you.

Lights on and off.

a diary – given to you

Dance. Dance. Dance.

a diary – given to you

a diary – given to you

-
Coma

a diary – given to you

coma

We need a code for when we are older.
Or if one of us loses the ability to speak,
Or if one of us is in a coma.

> *Karolina…*

How about this?
Tap. Tap. Tap.

> *And then?*

Three taps mean I love you.
Tap – I.
Tap – Love.
Tap - You.

You tap me all over. We laugh.

I love you more, I say.
We need a code for that too.

You tap me three times and stroke one
finger away.

Tap. Tap. Tap. – I love you
Stroke – more.

I smile.

That'll do.

a diary – given to you

broken hands

My phone rings.

Hey… he's in the hospital.
We'll come right now and pick you up.

caretaker.

I would do it all over again, you know?
It's not something I regret.

With two broken hands you can't do much.
You can't eat. You can't brush your teeth.
Sometimes the pain won't even let you
sleep.

Scared that I'll move the wrong way
Kick you in my sleep.
I tell you that I'll sleep on the floor.

You tell me: No, it's okay. You can stay.

Regardless, I grab the guest mattress,
place it next to you and tell you:
I love you. It's okay.

a diary – given to you

Routine follows suit.
I dress you and brush your hair too.
The days pass, and I write your essays too.

One day as we lay in bed, you tell me:

> Karolina... I'll never forget this.
> You being here for me –
> Doing all of this.
>
> I'll never forget that.
>
> Thank you.

a diary – given to you

before rem

I loved talking to you,
Especially right before we would fall asleep.

I told you about all my coursework, the
latest gossip, my hopes, and my dreams.

Hands moving frantically as I explain action
potentials to you.

I asked you about yours.
Listened attentively, as you told me about
your dreams of starting your own company.

I believed in your visions. I still do.

We would drift in conversations
from neuroscience
to the stock market
to the cheesy book, I just read.

a diary – given to you

We would talk about it all. But sometimes
you would interrupt me and say:

> *Can we lay in silence for a bit?*
> *You can lay on my chest.*

I nod
Head on your chest
Move to see a glimpse of your face.

You would smile, shake your head
And say:

> *Let's just dream for a little bit.*

a diary – given to you

confession

Remember how I used to tell you to sit in
silence with me before we would go to
sleep?

Yeah, I do.

Do you want to know why?

Before those moments of silence,
I would see your face light up as you talked
about everything that interested you.

I loved listening to you.

And in those moments of silence that I
asked for,
I would imagine…

a diary – given to you

Where we would be.
What we would have.
Happy and proud to have you by my side.

I wanted to fall asleep dreaming.
Hoping that *they* have just as much passion
as you do.

Just as curious as you were when you
looked up at me to see if I was already
asleep.

That was my favorite part of the day.

Just to dream,
with you by my side.

a diary – given to you

a diary – given to you

-

A Mirror of Us

a diary – given to you

a diary – given to you

plant

A gift to us,
Something green and bright,
Something alive

Once full of color
Once full of life

It withered away.

A mirror of us.

a diary – given to you

february 4th

Days were slow, and we fell into a routine.
That day, I was supposed to cook dinner for
you and your family.
I was excited, and so were you.

Let's add this. Let's add wine.
Maybe add this too.

You laugh. You chuckle.
And pull me close.

> *I love you.*
> *I love living with you.*

---

a diary – given to you

2 hours later.
I lay on the floor.

Your phone in hand.

Hands trembling. My heart racing.

Run to the bedroom.
Grab my clothes
Knowing I have to go.

Your eyes in shock.
You cry out:.

>It was one kiss.
>It was *only* a kiss.

a diary – given to you

a diary – given to you

-
Help Me

a diary – given to you

what did I say?

Shut door.
Hands shake.
I tremble with fear.

Was I being too noisy?
Did I overstep a boundary?

But he was acting weird.
He's never acted like that before.

Who's that girl?
Pretty brown long hair.

Why is her number not saved?

Why did he cry
Lash out
And walk away?

Maybe I shouldn't have acted that way.
Is it my fault?
What did I say?

a diary – given to you

help me

I'm outside.
I need your help.
Please.
I need your help.

All I see is blood.
Torn skin.

Swollen hands and bloody knuckles.

I bring you to the bathroom.
Pour cold water on your wounds.

It hurts. It hurts.

I know. I know.
But you'll be okay.

a diary – given to you

what can be so bad

A cold towel placed on your hands.
To make the swelling go down.
Ease the blood pouring down.
I look into your tired eyes and sigh..

What can be so bad?

a diary – given to you

safe haven

You tell her your secrets
How you've been feeling.

She calms you down.
A safe haven that I couldn't be.

I put the phone down.
Look up at you and say:

I'm sorry.
I'm so so sorry.

It's okay.

a diary – given to you

kitchen table

How was it?

You hide your knuckles.
But when you grab your fork, your mother
takes notice.

Your brother too.

What happened?

What do I say?
I invaded his privacy.
And full of rage and fear.
He hit a tree.

Came back with bloody knuckles,
And begged me:

help me.

a diary – given to you

-
Manipulation

a diary – given to you

I believed you

You promised me.
And I believed you.

a diary – given to you

february 4th part two

4 months later,
4 months too late.
4 months into living with you.

I find the messages.

The ones you hid.
The ones you deleted, too.

a diary – given to you

truth

You left and hit a tree.
Came back with blood on your hands.
Making me feel guilty.

Allowing me to take care of you,
Selectively deleted the messages.
So, it only seemed like she was there for you.

You lied to me.
Blatantly —
lied to my face.

No remorse.
Made me feel guilty for invading your
privacy.

Why did you lie to me?
Why didn't you just tell me then?
Why put me through that?

Why move in with me a month later,
knowing you lied to me?

All I did was beg for the truth.
Over and over and over again, I asked you if
you cheated.
You promised me you didn't.

Why?
Why lie to me?

a diary – given to you

a diary – given to you

a diary – given to you

–
Worthless

nightmare

To have looked into the eyes of a person
who once loved you beyond despair.
To have looked into the eyes of that same
person who now looks at you with despair.

Knowing that there is no love —
Nothing there

My worst nightmare.

your answer

It's because I didn't want to lose you.

And now you do?

It's different now.

Now I don't love you.

a diary – given to you

a diary – given to you

–
Mornings without you

a diary – given to you

first night

You left.

I lay in our bed.
Lay in the middle.
Try to fill up the space.
Make the emptiness go away.

Close my eyes and repeat the images in my
head:
You and her.
You and her.
You and me.

It was you and her.

Open my eyes and stay awake.
Cry for hours until there's nothing left.

I toss and turn.
Move blankets —
Pillows too.

Try sleeping upside down.

But nothing was worse
Than waking up without you.

a diary – given to you

collapse

My whole-body cold.
Trembling and anxiety-ridden.

I stumble out of bed.
Too tired to stay awake.
Too tired to sleep again.

I move towards the kitchen.
K-cup in.
Wait for the hissing of the machine.

Grab a cup and stare blankly at the wall.

I don't know what I'm going to do.
I don't know who to call.
What to say.
I'm here alone.
I don't know where to go.

I feel so alone.

I move towards the bedroom.
Coffee in hand.

I collapse.
I scream.
I welp.

I need to leave.

bathroom floor

I still remember the coldness of the floor.
How uninviting it felt.

My body crumpled,
I fall into myself,
Wrap my arms around my body.

Tears shower down faster than I can catch.

Breathing became a task to do.
So overwhelmed
By the thought of you.

On the bathroom floor, I lay.

a diary – given to you

a diary – given to you

a diary – given to you

Memories

a diary – given to you

blue glasses

I walk into the kitchen

Look at the fridge.
A picture of us in Milan,
Verona too.

I walk into the living room, Malaga too.

Open the cupboard,
See those shiny blue glasses.

The first time I met your parents.
The one's they gave us when we moved in
together.

a diary – given to you

Their fragility daunts me.
I grab them one by one
Throw them all on the floor.
Fragile blue pieces everywhere.

Move to the fridge, tear the pictures apart.
Grab the picture of Malaga –
Throw it against the wall.

I breathe.

Head towards the bedroom
Grab the vacuum.

And breathe.

collectives

Any place travelled
Any place seen.

I would collect
Anything and everything.

My favorite ones would be tickets:

Bus tickets
Train tickets
Museums.

Anything that marked a specific point in
time.

A ticket to travel back in time.

a diary – given to you

the alchemist

My favorite book is the Alchemist.
I read it when I was sixteen.
At seventeen too
At eighteen, I gave it to you.

All highlighted and notes inside.

Personalized to my interpretation.
A diary – given to you.

The day you finished it,
Eagerly and proudly

You say:

> *"So, I love you because the entire universe
> conspired to help me find you."*

a diary – given to you

Jan. @13. 8:07pm   18 : In love

It's hard ~~and~~ describing a love as pure
as ~~so~~ ours, without ~~it~~ feeling overbearing
for the ~~other~~ person.
~~outside~~ outside

I'm 18 and oh I am so in love. There is
no other person I could envision myself
with. ~~It's~~

I'm 18. Is that too young?

But... but... but

I'm 18 and I'm in love.

That's all that matters when
            you're 18 and in love.
                and
I'm sorry if that's overbearing.

It's just that I'm in love and
I can't stop sharing.

a diary – given to you

a million ways to meet you

I think about how we met
And how a million factors
played together to win that bet.

Moving to your city –
A place I've never met.

The little red house
Only a street down from yours.

The bus stop where I first saw you.

There were a million ways to meet you, and
that was one.

Maybe that's why I couldn't help,
But think that *you* were the one.

a diary – given to you

la vie en rose

There's always a defining piece in a
relationship.
It may be a song, a book, or a place.

Ours was *La Vie en Rose*.

Centered in a beautiful alley on a hot
summer night in Spain,

We sit across from other,
La vie en rose playing in the background.
My eyes bright
I tell you that it's my favorite song:

> *Quand il me prend dans ses bras*
> *Il me parle tout bas*
> *Je vois la vie en rose*
>
> *When he takes me into his arms,*
> *He speaks to me softly*
> *And I see life through rose-colored*
> *glasses.*

a diary – given to you

chocolate churros

We found a café.

One that sells the best chocolate churros in
town.

I dip my churro into the creamy chocolate.
Reach for my mouth,
Only for it to drip out.

I miss that laugh.
Your bright eyes
And the way you looked at me that day:

You chuckle and say,

>   *I could watch you the whole day.*
>   *I'm so glad I met you.*

Chocolate churro in my mouth,
I mumble.

>   *I love you too.*

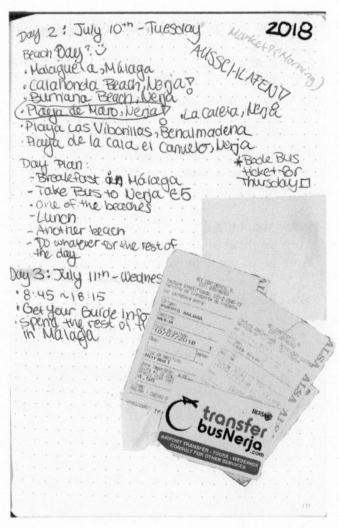

Day 2: July 10th - Tuesday   Market? (Morning)   **2018**
Beach Day? ☺   AUSSCHLAFEN
• Malagueta, Málaga
• Calahonda Beach, Nerja?
• Burriana Beach, Nerja
• Playa de Maro, Nerja   . La Calera, Nerja
• Playa Las Viborillas, Benalmadena
• Playa de la Cala el Canuelo, Nerja

Day Plan: * Book Bus
 - Breakfast in Málaga   ticket for
 - Take Bus to Nerja €5   Thursday ☐
 • One of the beaches
 - Lunch
 - Another beach
 - Do whatever for the rest of
   the day

Day 3: July 11th - Wednes
• 8.45 ~ 18.15
• Get Your Guide info
• Spend the rest of th
  in Málaga

Malaga Itinerary

a diary – given to you

kissing in the ocean

We place our towels on the beach.

And —
Swim to the middle of the ocean.
Let ourselves sink in.
Salty drained hair.

You pull me close.
Move my hair.
Touch my face.
Your hands on my neck.

And kiss me in the ocean.

a diary – given to you

a diary – given to you

white curtains

the sun set
long white curtains swing
the wind invites itself in.

clean white sheets,
my red dress slips off
and I fall into you.

utterly and completely.

I'm yours.
I whisper.
I'm yours.

Forever

Truly, yours.

compass

I gave you a necklace in the shape of a
compass.
On the back,
Our date engraved.

You told me,
You wore it to keep you safe.

a diary – given to you

polaroid

On my dorm bed,
I place the box.

A letter too.
Close your eyes, I tell you.

A polaroid camera just for you.
Soon you would go:

Take it to San Francisco
Colorado
Costa Rica
And Peru too.

Take it with you,
A polaroid –
Just for you.

graduation

Promise me —
You'll be there as I walk across that stage.

Promise me —
You'll be there to embrace me.

Promise me —
You'll be there to congratulate me.

I promise.

a diary – given to you

New Year's Eve 2018 ~~█████████~~ The restauran~~t~~
was called El Carnicero ~~████████~~

~~I loved that night.~~

We never took our eyes off of each other.

somewhere in Milan.

a diary – given to you

a diary – given to you

the beatles in mexico

Flies and sticky tables,

We walk in
Pictures of the Beatles are everywhere.
Any corner that you could think of...
There they were.

Then our food comes. He vanishes after that.

5 minutes later, music starts playing.
Ukulele in hand
Out of the kitchen
Black wig on head,
he begins:

> *One day, you'll look*
> *To see I've gone*
> *For tomorrow may rain, so*
> *I'll follow the sun.*

Bright eyes and big smile.
I grab my phone and press record.

He begins to sing even louder.

> *Someday, you'll know*
> *I was the one*
> *But tomorrow may rain, so*
> *I'll follow the sun.*

a diary – given to you

a diary – given to you

little tomatoes

Helmets flying off our heads

> *Karolina put it back on*
> *Oh my god*
> *Why did you rent this?*
> *We are going to die.*
> *Karolina hold on to me!*

I laugh.

Blazing heat.
Narrow highway.
Wind blinding our eyes.
I sit behind you, holding on tightly,
Giant trucks pass us.
Little cars too.

Finally, there
Scooter parked
We look at each other and laugh.

You poke my face -

> *Your face is SO red.*
> *Yours too!*

Faces swollen and burnt –
You take pictures

Two little tomatoes in Mexico.

a diary – given to you

coco

Stray black dog runs up to me.
I look around, but it continues to follow me.

I look to you.

I'm sure he has an owner.
He's well-fed
Groomed too.

We continue along the beach.
Stray or not, I'll play with him.

I call him Coco.
As you pull me to leave.

a diary – given to you

cocker spaniel

Not too small,
Not too tall.

Cute and curly,
A companion I've always wanted.

I tell you;
I want a Cocker Spaniel.

One that's ours.
One that we'll call Coco.

Coco the Cocker Spaniel.

a diary – given to you

a diary – given to you

shallow

I think I've found my new favorite song.

Show me.

I play the song. Clear my throat.
In the sha-ha-sha-ha-llow
In the sha-ha-sha-la-la-la-llow

You laugh.

Let's listen to it again, I say.
Again, and again and again.
Now we both sing, switching parts.

You look me in the eyes,
Begin singing loudly and deeply.

Tell me somethin', girl
Are you happy in this modern world?
Or do you need more?
Is there somethin' else you're searchin' for?

My smile reaches my eyes.

Together, we sing.

In the sha-ha-sha-ha-llow
In the sha-ha-sha-la-la-la-llow
In the sha-ha-sha-ha-llow
We're far from the shallow now

a diary – given to you

a diary – given to you

copenhagen

I had a layover in Copenhagen.

Except it was delayed.
The flight would be the next day.

So, I look for a hotel.

I'll come with you, you say.

No that's crazy. You can stay.

You grab your phone.
Search for my flight.

> *I want to spend one more day with you.*
> *Even if it's just one night in*
> *Copenhagen.*

You show me your screen.
It's booked.
One roundtrip.

> *Let's spend one more day together.*
> *One more day in Copenhagen.*
> *Just to be with you.*

guitar

You call me,
I've bought a guitar.

I'm going to learn that song of yours.
You know,

In the sha-ha-sha-ha-llow

For when you come back.
I'll know it by then.
I'll practice every day, you say.

I'll play it when you come back.

a diary – given to you

bookshelf

You had three bookshelves
Filled with books ranging from:

Architecture
Design
Psychology
And
Crime

I spent countless hours looking at them,
Reading through them,
Engaging in conversations about them.

It was my favorite part of your home.
I found comfort in them.
Stories that I could be a part of.

Even if I always knew,
They were never mine to claim.

I wonder now what books fill those shelves
What stories,
What conversations are struck.

Is there a memory of us?

a diary – given to you

a diary – given to you

-

Empty Spaces

a diary – given to you

a diary – given to you

I wake and the memories fade.
I'm surrounded by an empty space.

a diary – given to you

a diary – given to you

brillux

I moved here in 2017 and left the following
year.

Yet, I always came back.
Every two to three months I was here.

And slowly everything became familiar in a
way that I've never known.

Every drive into the city.
A marker that everyone knows —
That Brillux sign.

Bright and colorful.
The sign that marked —

You were close to *home*.

empty spaces

I grew up with empty spaces.
Moving in and filling everything to make it
a temporary home.
Only to survive for the next year or two,
And leave that temporary home —
An empty space.

It was what I was used to.
But with each passing year, I longed for a
full space.

A space full of memories.
A space that felt like home.
Somewhere grounded and not moved.

The street you grew up on.
The school you attended for years with
your childhood friends.
The actual growth one finds in a home.

A filled-up space.

I envied people who had such a space.

And then I met you.
With much hesitation, I resisted.

a diary – given to you

Afraid of what it would mean to build that
space around you.

I fought.
I broke up.
I screamed.
I cried.
I didn't want that space to be temporary.
I wanted it to feel like home.

But slowly, I began to believe your words.
Your repeated words that you would be
there —
Through the good and the bad.

You would make sure that I was happy.
That all you could ever want for me is to be
happy.

I cherished those words.
Devoured every inch of them that I could.

Maybe you would be the one to fill up that
space.

---

a diary – given to you

And so it happened.
It was fast. Convenient even.

We found an empty space.
Tore it apart. Made it ours.
And for the first time:

    I felt at *home.*

Lying next to you, your arms around mine.
In our filled-up space.
Filled with touches of you and me.
A space that was ours.
A space that I could call —

    Home.

a diary – given to you

Yet, in an instant

Like all the other spaces in my past:
We decorated it.
Furnished it.
Made it a home.
Only for it to be temporary.

No fight to keep it.
No attempt to repair the holes.
I had to leave yet again.
No choice given.

An empty space.

a diary - given to you

a diary – given to you

–
Thirty minutes

a diary – given to you

a diary – given to you

Is it easier to throw it all away?

a diary – given to you

a diary – given to you

take everything back

I gave almost everything back to you.
When you left me, I wanted to leave too —
Leave a part of me with you.

Necklace.
Watch.
Shirts.

Everything that reminded me of you.

door

When I asked you to fight,
Please, please
Fight.

You headed towards the door.
Looked at me one last time.

I don't love you anymore.
And shut the door.

a diary – given to you

-
One more day

a diary – given to you

february 14th

My heart tires as I write this.
Something I've tried to ignore,
But it always reminds me.

So, I write -
February 14th you came back,
Asked for one final goodbye.

I asked if we could take a walk.

The lake was frozen.
The first time since 1974.
I laughed and smiled as I glid across the ice.
A tired smile.
Turned around and looked at you.

This is beautiful.

You at a distance, watch me, and look away.

It was one of the most beautiful days.
For the ice froze and we could walk on
water.

It was one of the most painful days.
My last plea for you to stay,
knowing we both needed to walk away.

a diary – given to you

snowstorm

How ironic for us to end
When the snowstorm passed through.

How ironic for us to escape,
When the snowstorm trapped us in.

How ironic for us to love one last time.
Before the snowstorm took us away.

Our muffled sounds
Were all that remained.

a diary – given to you

the last time you saw me

The last time you saw me,
What did you see?

A broken version of me?

a diary – given to you

the last time I saw you

My eyes, full of fear
The taxi is here.

Fight for me, I think.
Please don't let me go

Please
Please
Please

Hold me one more time.
Kiss me one more time.

How could you let me go?
Where did all that love go?

a diary - given to you

a diary – given to you

-
Airports

a diary – given to you

a diary – given to you

simpler

It's two minutes past midnight.
My thoughts blurry.
My body heavy.
I sit in front of the gate.
Flight delayed.

I close my eyes,
And think of her.
You and her.

Did you see her and smile?
Was she kind and funny?

Did your hands touch hers?
Did your lips touch hers?
Were you happy then?
Relieved even?

Did you think of me?
Did you wish that was me?

Or were you glad that it was her?
A simpler,
Maybe —

Better version of me?

a diary – given to you

a diary – given to you

amsterdam

I am flying back to *our* airport.
The one where we had our reunions.

Only you won't be there
To smile and pick me up.

No more lies

A month after your lips touched hers
Yours were all over mine.
No remorse.
No shame.

I wish I never found out about that kiss.
And I wish you were here to pick me up.

To kiss my lips.
Make me forget.

Please.
Please.
Please.

Make me forget.

Her lips.

a diary – given to you

My eyes drift to sleep.
Maybe I wasn't exciting enough.

a diary – given to you

landing

The airplane lands.
A loud thud fills the plane.
I wake up.

I wish I could erase you.
Erase all of our memories.
And for once, not feel the pain of missing
you anymore.

Land somewhere, where we don't exist.

a diary – given to you

a diary – given to you

Love Addiction

a diary – given to you

cycles

I'm sorry. I love you.

I'll book a ticket and fly to you

Like I always did.

Or fly here
I'll pick you up.
We'll run away
And pretend this never happened

I'll love you like I always did.

I won't have any doubt.
I won't let you go like this.
I will fight for you over and over again.
Because I love you.

Like I always did.

I made a mistake.
I'm here now.
To fix it.
I'm here.
And I love you.

Like I always did.

---

a diary – given to you

And then I fall asleep
For a couple of hours of peace
Only to wake and realize that we didn't run
away.

And that you didn't beg me to stay.

a diary – given to you

at night

I wonder if you lay in bed at night and
think of me too.
I wonder if you think of me and long for me
when you do.

a diary – given to you

today

Some days I hate you —
I really do.
I hate you for what you did
And what you put me through.

But today, I love you.
I love you for your smile.
I love you for your laugh.
I love you for you.

Today, I love you.

Knowing that even on the days that I hate
you.
I'll love you just a little more.

hiccups

I know you miss my smile.
How I used to laugh
My chuckles
And hiccups too.

Hell, maybe you even miss my crazy
moods.

Maybe,
You miss my warmth
And my coldness too.

But I think you'll miss the most:
How much I believed in you.

a diary – given to you

a diary – given to you

replaceable

You miss the parts of me
That you can find in other people.

But I know you don't miss me
Not nearly as much as I miss you.

a diary – given to you

I should have believed you

Tears in your eyes
You tell me what happened.

How you lied
How you cheated
On the girl before me

And how it kills you inside.

> *I'm scared that I'll do it to you too*
> *You don't deserve that, you say.*

Well, if you love me, then don't hurt me

I'm scared that I'll do it to you too,
You say
Over
And over
And over again.

And then I console
I tell you that it will be alright
That I trust you.

3 years later –
I sit here and write.

I should have believed you.

picking flowers

You're not my responsibility anymore.

Yes.

Yes, I want to meet other people.

Accept it.

Move on.

I don't love you anymore.

I don't see myself being happy with you anymore.

I do love you.

I don't know.

I don't know if I love you.

I miss you.

You make me so happy.

I'm sorry.

I don't know what I want.

I love you.

a diary – given to you

I'll be lonelier with you than without you.

a diary – given to you

to be loved

You could have told me anything.
I don't think it would have changed a thing.

Because no matter what you did
Or what you said.

I wanted *so badly* to be loved.

a diary – given to you

-
Mein Herz
My Heart

mein herz

Your name became my heart.
Figuratively and intentionally.

Your name —
Always calling you —

Mein Herz.

a diary – given to you

I think the favorite part of me,

was you.

a diary – given to you

through you

You used to tell me -
If only you could see yourself as I do

I did -
I fell in love with me through you.
Loved who I was with you.

So, when you left,
Not only did I lose you
I felt like I lost the best part of myself.

The version I came to love —
Through you.

a diary – given to you

-
Unrecognizable

a diary – given to you

For a while, you made me a woman I never wanted to become.

I wonder when I'll stop counting the days.

part of me

The bad part of me.

I think part of me likes feeling this sadness.
It's the only way I'll feel close to you
anymore.
Maybe if I'm sad,
Maybe if I'm completely broken,

That energy will transmit to you.
And you'll feel it,
Show up
Ready to pick me up
Ready to fight.

Maybe sadness is the only way I'll stay
connected to you.
And sometimes I would rather feel that
pain.
Than to let you go

I hate that part of me.

a diary – given to you

why do you control me?

Oh, how I love you.
Oh, how I hate you.

You keep me up late at night.
Wake me up on those uninviting mornings.

Always wanting more
Always monitoring
Always pushing you away

Oh, how I love you.
Oh, how I hate you.

My only feeling of control.

Why do you control me?

Food.

loving half of you

I can't help but think of you.
Not the person you are today,

But my version of you:
What happens when that version is only
partly true?
Can I only love half of you?

Or maybe I never loved you at all,
because loving a version of you is not the
same as loving you.

Yet I do.
I do love you.
Even if I only love half of you.

a diary – given to you

a diary – given to you

-

What if the person that hurt me was hurting too?

a diary – given to you

I wasn't the only one

I know I write about how it was always so
easy for you.

How you told me that you no longer loved
me
How you wanted to leave.

But that's only partly true.
The part that I didn't mention –
The part I refused to say.

You had a hard time letting go too.

Everything –
It took too much out of you.

a diary – given to you

avalanche

Our methods of love were opposite.
You loved at first sight
I loved you most at last.

You fell quickly.
I fell slowly.

A gradual avalanche –
Overwhelming both you and me.

addiction

When we would fight,
Scream and cry.

Only for it to all be all right
As we lay side by side.

One day confessing, you say:

I was so addicted to you,
To that feeling that everything will be okay.

Please understand, I don't ever want to feel that
way.

impossible

It wasn't that you never fought.
You fought.
For a long time, that's all you did.

And I understand,
For the first time, I understand
That it was tiring.

It was tiring fighting for someone that had
no certainty and stability.

It wasn't impossible.
We always made it work.

But when that trust is gone
To fight for someone
You've fought for so long.

Seems far gone.

easy

I realize that loving me wasn't always easy.
I know my moods made you sad too.

And for that, I'm sorry.
I realize sometimes I was too much for you.

a diary – given to you

Maybe writing about you wasn't about forgetting.

a diary – given to you

Maybe it was all about forgiving.

a diary – given to you

Healing

eyes

What makes you want to stay?
After the lies and the hurt.
Why would you want to stay?
Why beg him?

It was simple, really —
When you look into the eyes of someone
you love,
And no matter the pain you've been
through,

When you look into their eyes,
And you can't look away —
Becomes the best reason to stay.

I choose you

People always talk about the perfect
partner.
The one that completes you.

I hate that idea.
Love isn't perfect, and it's never complete.

Sometimes it's chaotic.
Maybe hurtful too.

But I like to think that

When you look at the person in front of
you…
Notice their flaws and imperfections too.

You would still say:

I choose you

a diary – given to you

▓▓▓▓▓▓▓▓▓▓▓▓▓▓▓▓▓▓▓▓▓▓▓▓▓▓ . Hell, they even proved to you how much they loved you. They weren't all that bad. They were there for you when you had no one. They held you in your arms when you felt absolutely broken inside.

And then... you find out their secret. you confront them. you scream. you cry. you insult. you become numb. ▓▓▓▓▓▓▓▓▓▓▓▓▓▓▓▓▓▓▓▓▓▓▓▓▓ ▓▓▓▓▓▓▓▓▓▓ you feel betrayed. like every touch and kiss from the moment he cheated was a lie.

▓▓▓▓▓▓▓▓▓▓▓▓▓▓▓▓▓▓▓▓▓▓▓▓▓ ▓▓▓▓▓▓▓▓▓▓▓▓▓▓▓▓▓▓▓▓▓ ▓▓▓▓▓▓▓▓▓▓▓▓▓▓ you know deep down that love isn't supposed to be like this ▓▓▓▓▓▓▓▓

a diary – given to you

again

I would like to feel like what it is like to be
wanted again
To have someone's hand trickle down my
back.

I would like to feel like what it is like to be
kissed again
Passionate lips wanting more.

I would like to feel like what it is like to be
loved again.
Your warmth transcending through me
without ever once touching me.

That's what I truly want.
To be kissed again
To be loved again
To feel everything again

But for the first time–
I would like to feel like what it's like to be
loved —

Without you.

remnants

The pain eventually subsided.
There were still remnants of you:
A song heard
A word said
I would go back to you

But the pain subsided
Until I found myself

No longer in love with you.

a diary – given to you

\-

Into Everything

into everything

I've tried everything to get over you.
Read through countless articles
Self-help books too.

But I found that -
It wasn't a matter of getting over you or us.

It was a matter of getting into everything
else in my life.

Be it, my family
My friends
My passions

And my writing.

That wouldn't have been possible had you
never left me.

control you

Healing doesn't mean that one day
I'll forget all about you.

Healing means dealing with the pain,
Crying when I need to
Screaming too.

Until one day, I find that it doesn't control
me.

a diary – given to you

I set time away to write about you, but today my mind escapes. The words don't come rushing out.
I think this a part of getting over you. The part where there's nothing left to say.

a diary – given to you

mirror

I looked at the mirror today.

For months I would hate what I saw –
This broken version of me.
This sadness and hate that built up inside of
me.

I looked at the mirror today.
And for the first time in a while –

      I'm proud of me

Proud of the woman that I have the
potential to be.

a diary – given to you

intense

I'm incredibly intense
And read into everything and anything.

But I love that part of me.
It's thoroughly and wholly –

Me.

a diary – given to you

when I'll read this again

5 years from now.
I'll probably read this again.

This book in hand.
A reminder of the woman I used to be.

I wonder where I'll be.
And who I'll be.

5 years from now –
I hope I'll be proud of me.

open arms

I don't want to fall into the arms of someone
else

To heal me
To fix me
To mend my broken heart

No —
I want to fall into myself.

A call to open arms —
You are home.

a diary – given to you

–

'A Home in the Heart'

–

The House on Mango Street

a diary – given to you

a diary – given to you

Hey it's Karo…

a diary – given to you

a diary – given to you

home

Home. Home. Home.

You tell me that I only loved you for this
concept of home.

You ask me.
Did you ever truly love me?
Or did you love the sense of home I gave?

Can you truly say that you loved me?
Tell me.

pieces

It wasn't until I laid it all out.
All the poems in front of me.

There was our story.
Not complete.
There were missing pieces,
Memories untold,
Memories forgotten

But with the pieces in front of me,
I found all the beauty and more.

Although chaotic and painful,
I was so vulnerable
And in vulnerability lies endless possibility.

So, I thank you.
A story unfinished,
I mark it an ending.

a diary – given to you

my answer

You were home for what I knew home was –
A home in the heart.

a diary – given to you

a diary – given to you

Thank you.

a diary – given to you

a diary – given to you

a diary – given to you

acknowledgements

To my parents, as much as we may fight and bicker, I adore and love you – forever.

To my family, you are everywhere — an accumulation of millions of miles away. Yet, despite that I always feel your love – no distance is too great.

To my friends, you all have been so patient with me. I'm lucky to have friends like you.

To Gerald and Sophie, a power couple that I adore. Thank you, Gerald, for being the first one to read my book and planting the courage in me to publish it. Thank you, Sophie, for your unwavering kindness.

To my readers, thank you for choosing to read this book. It means the world to me.

a diary – given to you

Index

a diary – given to you

a diary - given to you

a diary – given to you

a diary – given to you

a diary – given to you

Find out more about the author on:

karolinavalentina.com

Instagram: @karolinavalentina_

a diary – given to you

a diary – given to you

Find out more about the cover artist on:

kelletteworks.com

Instagram: @kelletteworks

Made in the USA
Coppell, TX
03 August 2021